Families

Grandparents

Rebecca Rissman

www.raintreepublishers.co.uk
Visit our website to find out
more information about
Raintree books.

To order:

☎ Phone 0845 6044371

🖷 Fax +44 (0) 1865 312263

🖵 Email myorders@raintreepublishers.co.uk

Customers from outside the UK please telephone +44 1865 312262

Raintree is an imprint of Capstone Global Library Limited, a company
incorporated in England and Wales having its registered office at 7 Pilgrim
Street, London, EC4V 6LB – Registered company number: 6695582

Text © Capstone Global Library Limited 2011
First published in hardback in 2011
Paperback edition first published in 2012
The moral rights of the proprietor have been asserted.

Edited by Rebecca Rissman, Dan Nunn, and Catherine Veitch
Designed by Ryan Frieson
Picture research by Tracy Cummins
Production by Victoria Fitzgerald
Originated by Capstone Global Library
Printed and bound in China by Leo Paper Products Ltd

ISBN 978 1 406 22148 0 (hardback)
14 13 12 11 10
10 9 8 7 6 5 4 3 2 1

ISBN 978 1 406 22156 5 (paperback)
15 14 13 12 11
10 9 8 7 6 5 4 3 2 1

British Library Cataloguing in Publication Data
Rissman, Rebecca.
Grandparents. -- (Families)
306.8'745-dc22

Acknowledgements
We would like to thank the following for permission to reproduce photographs:
Corbis pp.**10** (©Markus Moellenberg), **14** (©Kevin Dodge), **19** (©Nils Hendrik
Muller/Cultura), **20** (©Kristy-Anne Glubish/Design Pics), **23 c** (©Markus
Moellenberg); Getty Images pp. **4** (Sylvain Grandadam), **7** (Stephen Chiang),
8 (Tony Metaxas), **9** (Jupiterimages), **11** (Jay Reilly), **13** (Manoj Adlukay), **16**
(Ron Levine), **17** (Image Source), **18** (Alex Mares-Manton), **21** (Ariel Skelley),
23 a (Manoj Adlukay); istockphoto pp. **5** (©Ann Marie Kurtz), **22** (©Diane
Labombarbe); Photolibrary pp. **12** and **23 b** (both Radius Images); Shutterstock
pp. **6** (©Mehmet Dilsiz), **15** (©Yarek Gora).

Front cover photograph of a granddaughter kissing her grandmother
reproduced with permission of Getty Images (China Tourism Press). Back cover
photograph of a granddaughter helping her grandfather with his tie reproduced
with permission of Corbis (©Nils Hendrik Muller/Cultura).

We would like to thank Anne Pezalla, Dee Reid and Diana Bentley for their
invaluable help in the preparation of this book.

Every effort has been made to contact copyright holders of material reproduced
in this book. Any omissions will be rectified in subsequent printings if notice is
given to the publisher.

Contents

What is a family?

A family is a group of people who care for each other.

People in a family are different ages.

All families are different.

All families are special.

What are families like?

Some families like to play games.

Some families like to cook together.

Who are grandparents?

In a family there are parents. Parents are adults who have children.

grandparent

Parents have parents, too!

They are called grandparents.

Different grandparents

Your parent's mother is
your grandmother.

Your parent's father is
your grandfather.

Some families have
many grandparents.

Some families have few grandparents.
Some families do not have any
grandparents.

Some grandparents live far from their families.

Some grandparents live with their families.

Some grandparents care for
their grandchildren.

Some grandchildren help care for their grandparents.

Some families visit their grandparents at special homes.

Do you have grandparents?

Family tree

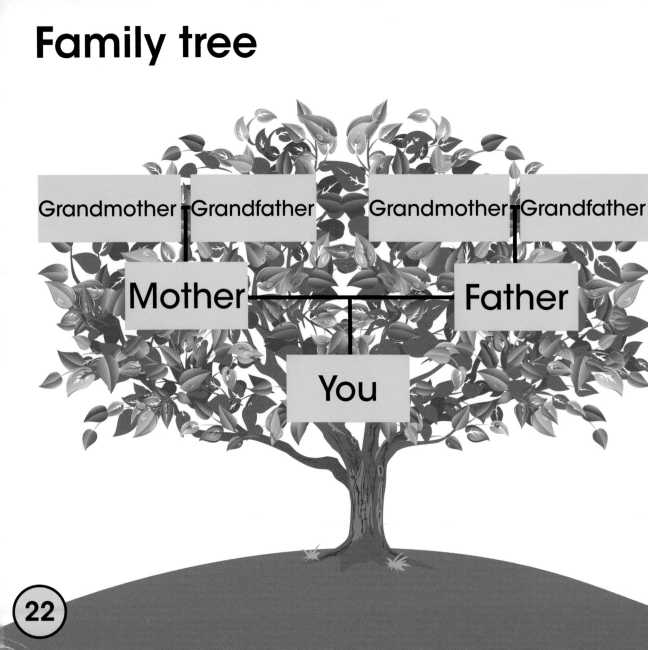

Grandmother · Grandfather · Grandmother · Grandfather · Mother · Father · You

Picture glossary

 **grandfather** a parent's father

 **grandmother** a parent's mother

 **parent** adult who has children

Index

Note to parents and teachers
Before reading
Explain to children that people in families are often related to each other. Most children are related to their parents. And parents have parents, too! They are a child's grandparents!

After reading
Ask children if they have special nicknames for their grandparents, such as Granny or Grandpa. Make a list of these names on the board.